Original title:
Growth on the Windowsill

Copyright © 2025 Creative Arts Management OÜ
All rights reserved.

Author: Nash Everly
ISBN HARDBACK: 978-1-80581-794-9
ISBN PAPERBACK: 978-1-80581-321-7
ISBN EBOOK: 978-1-80581-794-9

Fragrant Promises of Home

The basil whispers, 'More sun, please!'
While catnip schemes a feline tease.
Mint dreams of mojitos, so bold,
Stirred with laughter, stories told.

Chives stretch high to catch a glance,
While thyme, in green, begins to dance.
A pot of parsley rolls its eyes,
'You call this growth? What a surprise!'

The Joyful Strain of New Beginnings

A sprout pops up, with a cheer and a grin,
Stretching its leaves, wanting to win.
'Look at me!' it shouts with glee,
'I swear I'm not just a weed, you see!'

The sun peeks in, quite the joker,
Tickling the leaves of the little smoker.
Water drips down, a playful prank,
'Thirsty?' said the bidet, 'Be frank!'

Roots Tucked Beneath Glassy Facades

Beneath the surface, they wiggle and squirm,
Root secret agents, holding firm.
They gossip of soil, rich and grand,
While plotting world domination, so planned.

In pots so cozy, they knit their own socks,
Whispering tales of old gardening clocks.
'Let's sprout a plan, without a care,
No one can catch us, they don't dare!'

Oasis of Serenity on the Edge

Beyond the glass, a jungle at play,
Jade plants partying, in a leafy ballet.
Soft leaves sway, with a whimsical grin,
Dancing away, 'Let the fun begin!'

The clock ticks slow, but the plants don't mind,
In a world of green, joy intertwined.
Still, they giggle at the dusty cactus,
'What a prickly friend, so fantastical!'

Tender Shoots of Tomorrow

Tiny sprouts peek out to play,
Dancing leaves in a sunny ballet.
Each little plant wears a bright grin,
Whispering secrets of where they've been.

A stubborn cactus loves to jest,
While a basil sings, 'I'm the best!'
With every drop of rain that falls,
They throw a party in their small walls.

Sunlit Serenity

Lemon balm cozies up to the sun,
While mint is busy having fun.
Pansies laugh at the clouds above,
As they sip sweet nectar, feeling love.

Petunias strut in colorful attire,
Acting like divas who never tire.
A rogue sprout claims the windowsill throne,
Declaring, 'This light is all my own!'

Verdant Aspirations

Herbs in pots plot a grand scheme,
Dreaming of salads with a side of cream.
Thyme gives sage a cheeky poke,
While dill tries to pass off a joke.

A parsley sprig with pompous flair,
Claims the sunlight as if it's rare.
Yet every day, they know for sure,
Their time to shine is what they adore.

Awakening in Stillness

Morning dew on the leaves will dance,
As blossoms sway in nature's trance.
A sunflower yawns, stretching wide,
While kitchen herbs chat, side by side.

Chives gossip about their next meal,
Competing for who's the biggest deal.
In this leafy world, laughter's a must,
Each plant with dreams and a bit of trust.

Buds of Hope

Tiny leaves leap with glee,
Dancing on a tiny spree.
Sunlight bounces off the glass,
While neighbors walk on by, alas!

Fingers crossed for blooms so bold,
But first, I need to stop the mold.
A little water for a little laugh,
Maybe next time, I'll check the staff!

Chirping birds give me the scoop,
On all the gossip on this troop.
Sprouts whisper secrets, swap their tales,
While I'm just waiting for the snails!

I think I heard them plotting schemes,
To grow a forest from my dreams.
All this buzz from a pot so small,
Looks like they're having a ball!

Tending to Dreams

Tiny sprouts and pots so round,
In this wild jungle, I am crowned.
Watering cans become my throne,
As I converse with seedlings grown.

They say, 'Why fret? Let's stretch and play!'
With leaves like arms, they sway and sway.
A dance party in morning's beam,
The sun and I plot our grand scheme!

With soil on my shoes, I sweat and sigh,
Yet hope's my perfume, oh my, oh my!
Each leaf grins like it knows a joke,
And here I stand — no need for smoke!

Planting a vision, oh so sly,
I've just joined the greenhorn high!
Tomorrow's dreams sprout in a wink,
But today, I'll just let them think!

Resilience in the Light

Beams of sunlight, strong and bright,
Courage blossoms, oh what a sight!
Even weeds join the morning dance,
As pots of dreams take their chance.

Water with a side of jest,
The plant says, 'Just trust your best!'
A leaf flaps, a flower's wink,
Who knew they could make me think?

Every droplet, a hopeful shower,
I giggle, watching them tower.
Potted wonders, on the rise,
With funny faces, they mesmerize!

They thrive on light, or so they claim,
Learning life's silly little game.
I swear I heard my cactus tease,
Saying, "Life's easier with just a breeze!"

The Secret Life of Potted Souls

Oh, what secrets lie below?
In little pots where visions grow.
A fern says, "Life's a comedy!"
While sharing tales of a tragedy.

A rogue thyme braids with basil fair,
While novice sprouts from everywhere.
They whisper dreams of being grand,
Yet worry about our nature band!

"Do we take root or dance in air?
Is it cooler here, or over there?"
Laughter echoes, a floral spree,
In every pot, there's laughter, you see!

Cherishing dirt, a fragrant club,
We gather for a sunny grub.
With every laugh, we share our heart,
In potted souls, we're never apart!

A Symphony of Green in the Mundane

A pot of herbs sits by the sink,
Basil dreams while I just think.
Thyme's a joker, just grows tall,
Parsley giggles through it all.

A cactus waving like a hand,
Wondering if it should take a stand.
Mom's geraniums practice their sway,
Salsa dancing in a carefree way.

Dandelions plotting a heist,
In a fern's shade, they feel enticed.
Spaghetti squash thinks it's a star,
But it's stuck here, not going far.

Despite the confines, they thrive with glee,
Potted rebels, wild and free.
In this small world, they have their say,
Making the mundane a bright ballet.

Wild Spirits in Captive Spaces

A sunflower peeks through the glass,
Wondering if it can break the mass.
"Oh, to roam by the garden gate,"
It sighs, feeling a tad irate.

Mint's been planning a grand escape,
Plotting its journey with all the tape.
Chives chuckle with every sprout,
While the poor pansies just pout.

Tiny roots tickle the soil,
Hoping one day they'll feel the toil.
But for now, they lounge on a sill,
Snickering at the gardening thrill.

Mossy whispers make bathroom sounds,
While lily pads play in surrounding bounds.
Despite their limits, they live and bloom,
And fill this space with life's sweet zoom.

Roots in the Sunlight

A little pot of avocados waits,
Dreaming of brunch, it contemplates.
"Often I wish to split and fly,
But here I stay, oh my, oh my!"

Tomatoes blush in the morning light,
Chasing the sun with all their might.
"Do we need a vacation?" asks thyme,
As they sprout up, feeling sublime.

A spider plant spins tales of dreams,
Wishing on window sunbeams.
"Out in the wild, we'd dance and sway,
But for now, it's just us at play."

With roots entwined in a confined space,
They giggle and plunge at their own pace.
In this sunny nook, they've found delight,
Cheering each other, in shared sunlight.

Tiny Leaves Ascending

Little leaves stretch out, so spry,
Whispering secrets to the sky.
"I can see a world so wide,"
Says a leaf with a giddy pride.

Bean sprouts pretending to be tall,
Asking each other, "Can we ball?"
Lettuce curls up, just cannot wait,
For the garden gate, it dreams of fate.

Potatoes are lurking, bold and sly,
Shooting their eyes, oh me, oh my!
"Someday we'll roll, just wait and see,
For now, we'll be crunchy, wild, and free."

These tiny greens make mischief fun,
While sunshine plays, and dances run.
In the stillness, their laughter swells,
Singing their stories from their little cells.

Harmonies of Growth

Tiny sprout with lofty dreams,
Reaches out for sunbeams.
A dance for light, oh what a sight,
Though the cat thinks it's a kite.

Water drops become a game,
Spilling out like wild fame.
Frogs croak tunes, while bugs hum beats,
Nature's concert, oh what feats!

Leaves do wiggle, bend, and sway,
Trying hard to find their way.
But when the wind comes blowing strong,
They just giggle, 'We can't be wrong!'

In the pot, they start to brawl,
Competing for the sunlight's call.
Yet in their pushes, shoves, and jokes,
They find the fun with all those folks!

The Guardian of Green Life

In a corner, all aloof,
Sat a plant, protecting its roof.
Watched my coffee spill with glee,
Said, 'That's fine, it's good for me!'

With a wink and leafy cheer,
It whispered secrets in my ear.
'Life's a mess, but do not fret,
I know a thing or two, you bet!'

When I forget, it gives a shout,
'Time for water, that's what I'm about!'
Yet if I leave the pot too dry,
It rolls its eyes and gives a sigh.

Together, we share this space,
A leafy pal in a warm embrace.
For every quirk that makes me grin,
My guardian green always lets me win!

Serenity in the Struggle

A leaf unfurls, yet bends in jest,
Waves to the neighbor, doing its best.
But when the sun gets too intense,
It squints a bit, all in suspense.

Roots dig deep, beneath the soil,
Whispering tales of endless toil.
Yet every twist and turn they take,
Leads to laughter, no mistake!

A bug comes by with munching plans,
While the plant just wiggles and stands.
'You think I'm scared? Oh, take a bite!
I've got all day, I'm in for the fight!'

Rain drops drip with rhythmic cheer,
Each splash drops laughter near and dear.
Through trials thick and lessons wide,
They share smiles, their joyful stride!

Budding Aspirations

A sprout stands tall with dreams so bright,
Whispers, 'Watch me take to flight!'
Though a squirrel gives a teasing glance,
It laughs, 'Oh come on, give me a chance!'

With every inch towards the sky,
It shouts, 'So close! Oh my, oh my!'
A little bird then chirps with grace,
'You've got this, keep up the race!'

The sun peeks in through curtained glass,
While shadows dance, they twirl and pass.
And as the pot begins to shake,
The plant just snickers, 'For fun's sake!'

But wisdom's seed within it grows,
'Embrace the journey, that's how it goes.'
With every leaf that springs anew,
It nods and grins, 'You can too!'

Small Wonders of the World

Tiny sprouts in the sun,
Dancing like they're having fun.
Who knew that dirt could be chic?
With each leaf, they play hide-and-seek?

A pot filled with green and glee,
Whispers secrets, just for me.
A little basil looks so grand,
Plotting to spice up dinner plans!

Tomatoes giggle, red and round,
In this jungle, joy abounds.
With herbs and greens, I take a bow,
A farmer's hat? I'll wear it now!

So raise a toast to this little crew,
With wormy tales, they'll tell you too.
For in each leaf lies a tale so sweet,
Of the wonders found in a sunny seat.

Green Dreams in Concrete

Concrete jungles, but don't you fret,
A little green is a safe bet.
Poking through cracks, they wave and cheer,
Who knew life could be so near?

A dandelion in a gutter's snare,
Guess who's playing hide and share?
With every breeze, a dance of glee,
Look at me, I'm wild and free!

The city grumbles, but not our leaves,
In whimsical fashion, the plant life weaves.
Rosemary's whispering to the car horns,
"Keep your noise, I'll bloom at dawn's."

So here's to the green amidst the gray,
Watch them thrive in their cheeky way.
They'll teach us all how to be bold,
In this patch of land the stories unfold.

Life's Fragile Flourish

A sprig of thyme in a coffee cup,
Dreaming of gardens where it can strut.
Oh, see the mint, so sly and spry,
Says, "Mix me in; you won't deny!"

Tiny petals on the sill,
Waving at the world with sheer will.
Butterflies giggle and bees conspire,
In this corner, our hearts aspire!

A little pot that dances bright,
In morning sun, it's quite a sight.
But who knew it needed a rain check?
A splash of water or a neck-wreck?

So here's to life with twist and spin,
Where every pot holds a buddy within.
A fragile flourish, a comic scene,
In every little leaf, joy can be seen.

Roots in the Horizon

Tiny roots stretch far and wide,
Searching for mischief, they cannot hide.
"Where's the horizon?" one leaf asks,
With dreams of traveling, what a task!

In a pot, they plot and scheme,
To reach the skies, it's quite the dream!
An adventurous sprout with a dash of sass,
Sips morning dew from an empty glass.

They humor all with floppy hats,
Entwined together, gossiping chat.
"Look at us, we've got our flair!"
In our little world, we're the fairest of fare!

So here's a toast to roots so spry,
And how they reach to touch the sky.
With laughter in leaves and joy in sight,
Our tiny jungle feels just right.

Gentle Growth

A sprout peeks through the dirt,
With ambitions somewhat curt.
It stretches long to reach the light,
While dodging shoes that loom in sight.

A tiny leaf begins to dance,
Nearby, a raindrop takes its chance.
The sunbeam gives a cheerful grin,
"Keep stretching, friend, let the fun begin!"

In a pot that's way too small,
A herb declares, "I'm on a roll!"
With roots all tangled, it won't quit,
It dreams of salad—what a hit!

Tiny plants hold secret dreams,
Of being huge in grand regimes.
"Just keep your leaves up in style,"
Said the cactus with a spiky smile.

Secrets in the Soil

In the dirt, whispers abound,
Of veggies laughing underground.
A tater chips and says, "Oh dear,"
"I'm stuck down here, but let's have cheer!"

Worms wear shades, it's quite the sight,
Dancing in the late daylight.
They say, "We're all about the funk,
Turning scraps into our junk!"

The seeds keep plotting their escape,
Among the weeds, they plan and scrape.
One said, "Act cool, we've got this nailed,"
As the sunlight finally unveiled.

A pot of soil, full of tales,
Beneath the dirt, the laughter sails.
A loser's circle, yet who cares?
Tomorrow's lunch is all that shares!

Unfurling Dreams

A budding plant with big ideas,
Says, "I'll reach beyond my peers!"
It stretches out and strikes a pose,
While asking, "Which way does the wind blows?"

A leaf unrolls like a tight scroll,
A lesson learned, it took a toll.
"I planned a climb to heights so grand,
But got stuck under a cat's hand!"

The sun says, "Better stretch your frame,"
And winked at grass, "It's all a game."
Carrots giggled, "We're underground,
Our fashion's rad; we are profound!"

Spindly stalks form a conga line,
As roots invent the grand design.
With every twist, a side to see,
In a plant party, wild and free!

Emergence Amid Chaos

A seedling peeks through cloudy skies,
Amid the mess, it wears a guise.
Surrounded by a half-eaten snack,
Its little leaf tries to get back on track.

A dandelion shouts, "No fear,"
"Blow me, baby, make me clear!"
While sunflowers laugh at their own height,
"I'll block your sun, but it's alright!"

The chaos blooms in shades of glee,
Yet goes unnoticed, don't you see?
In pots so clustered, life's a race,
But all the weeds just want a space!

Tiny roots weave a merry song,
Despite the noise, they grow quite strong.
"Next time, don't blow me away, friend,"
A brave new bud said, "Let's pretend!"

Breaths of Fresh Air

Tiny leaves peek through the glass,
Doing the tango, moving fast.
Sunshine giggles, giving a wink,
Plants breakdance while I just blink.

Dust bunnies scatter, feeling the heat,
A basil plant rocking to the beat.
Chive chats loudly, with a green pout,
'I'm much wiser than you, no doubt!'

The tiny pot throws a wild bash,
Cacti yell, 'We may be brash!'
Sassy flowers shake their heads tight,
Who knew a sprout could feel so right?

Moss joins in, with a fuzzy roar,
'We're growing, but what's in store?'
While I sip tea and watch this spree,
I wonder who's the wildest, me or thee?

Cascades of Color and Life

A riot of colors fills the view,
Red, yellow, green - oh, what a crew!
The violets giggle, 'Is this a show?'
The daffodils nod, 'Just watch us grow!'

Pothos boasts of its shiny dress,
'Even in shade, I'll never stress!'
While succulents smirk in their prickly ways,
'We thrive in drought, just count the days!'

The old teapot's team is quite the sight,
Filled with herbs, shining day and night.
The rosemary leans with flair and grace,
'It's a garden party—let's save a place!'

Window whispers entice them to sway,
'Let's dance until the end of day!'
With laughter and cheer, they take a stand,
A party of plants, that's simply grand!

Vine and Twig

Twisting and turning, the vine goes bold,
Sticking its tongue out, never to fold.
'Twig, oh twig, lend me your hand,'
'Let's swing together, isn't it grand?'

With a nod and a creak, the twig complies,
Together they plot beneath sunny skies.
'We'll climb to the top, no room for doubt,'
'Let's leave this windowsill, and head out!'

A flock of pigeons jeers from above,
'You think you're daring, with all that love?'
But the vine just giggles, and wiggles away,
It's the thrill of the chase that makes them play!

As night descends, a moonlit cheer,
Nature's concert is what we hear.
With a skip and a jump, they sway and cling,
Oh, the mischief of twig and vine in spring!

Stretching Toward the Light

In the morning sun, a leafy cheer,
Plants reach up high, 'We're pioneer!'
With stems all tangled, in a twisty plight,
They mime a stretch, what a silly sight!

Each lily pad takes a bow so grand,
'Who knew sunlight could be so planned?'
While the mint argues on who's in charge,
'My smell's more potent, I'm the plant at large!'

Roses blush, showing their petals wide,
'Beauty's a game, it's all in the stride!'
Plants giggle softly, swaying with glee,
Winning the sunlight, their main decree.

As night falls, they settle and sigh,
What a peculiar sunny day gone by.
In the dance of leaves under silver hue,
Like little stars, in their pot of blue!

Flickers of Life in Forgotten Spaces

Tiny sprout in a cup with no flair,
Hiding behind dusty old teddy bear.
Reaching for sun with all of its might,
Wondering if it's a plant or a kite.

Sipping water like a cocktail diva,
Wishing for rain, not just a river.
Its leaves dance with joy, a clumsy ballet,
Spices up life in the oddest of ways.

A cheeky cousin of the garden crew,
Thinking it's time for a jungle review.
Potted dreams in a world far too bright,
Bringing fresh laughter, a sheer delight.

While neighbors stare with perplexed looks,
This leafy joke's got everyone hooked.
Living alone, just a bit of a tease,
A botanical stand-up, aiming to please.

The Miniature Jungle Affair

A tiny jungle in a coffee mug,
With a snail as a guide and a mug as a rug.
Cacti in bow ties, dressed for a show,
Both a jungle and a fashion faux pas, though!

Glancing at passersby with a wink,
"Join my tea party, come have a drink!"
Leaves gossip about the latest sprout,
Not the usual bloom, but that's what it's about!

When the light hits just right, they stretch and sway,
"It's plant fashion week! Hip-hip-hooray!"
Vines tangled like those messy old cords,
Turning this mug into a world of awards.

So sip your coffee, but don't dare to miss,
The plants on the run, cultivating bliss.
In each nook and cranny, life finds a way,
Making each morning feel like a holiday.

Transformation in a Small Frame

In an old frame that once held a smile,
A tendril peeks out, has been here a while.
It whispers to dust, "I'm a guest here, too,"
While plotting a coup for a better view.

With sunlight as paint, it colors the room,
While residents chuckle, "There goes the bloom!"
Socks as its neighbors—they sigh and complain,
"Who needs a decorator, let's go insane!"

Transformed by the light, roots striking a pose,
"Who knew a pot could look like this? Who knows?"
It beams with pride, feeling ever so grand,
A floral comedian with a sly masterplan.

In the laughter of life, it finds its own way,
Creating a magic in a mundane display.
So here's to the odd, the playful, the weird,
In every small frame, a miracle steered.

Verdant Dreams in Urban Cracks

Between asphalt cracks, a hero appears,
With leaves so bright, it cheers up the peers.
"Don't mind the concrete, I'm here to say,
That life finds a way, no matter the day!"

Grass sneezes from pollen, with a giggly sound,
"Excuse me, dear world, but look what I've found!"
As cars rush by, they glance in surprise,
At this bold little green that refuses to die.

In hats made of raindrops, it takes the stage,
Can't help but laugh at this urban rage!
Every inch of concrete is just part of the game,
With roots that shout loudly, "We're not feeling lame!"

So here's to the quirks, the brave in the cracks,
Living their dreams while dodging the tracks.
A surreal comedy, they laugh and grow wide,
Urban mishaps won't keep them inside!

Solstice of the Sprouts

In a pot, they dance and twirl,
Tiny leaves in a leafy whirl.
They squabble over sunlight's beam,
Plotting in their leafy dream.

One bean thinks it's a superstar,
Insisting it's the best by far.
While the basil rolls its eyes,
"I'm the herb that gets the prize!"

A cactus claims it's tough as nails,
With stories of its desert trails.
But the mint just giggles in delight,
"Try not to wilt in the moonlight!"

Together they sing, a motley crew,
In their pot, they've got quite the view.
A symphony of green on display,
Who knew plants could have such a play?

Harmony in Unlikely Places

A fern and a flower made quite the pair,
Trading gossip without a care.
A sprout quips, "You're taller than me!"
"Only by a leaf!" said the bumblebee.

Sunflowers turning to catch a wink,
"Oh, look at the clouds—they might just shrink!"
While the daisies giggle, oh so spry,
"Watch out, here comes a raindrop spy!"

Tomato plants wear a silly grin,
"Sometimes we lose, but we still win!"
They cheer each other, roots intertwined,
Creating bonds that are quite refined.

In this patch, oddballs do abound,
Nature's laughter is the sweetest sound.
From pot to plant, joy's the embrace,
Finding fun in this messy space!

Sun-Kissed Dreams in the City

From gritty bricks, sprouts poke their heads,
Defying all the concrete beds.
A tomato cries, "I want some sun!"
While the parsley says, "Let's have some fun!"

Pigeons scratch and give a glare,
As the chives wave without a care.
"Why do you strut? You've got no roots!"
The city plants in their fancy suits.

A sunflower winks at the city lights,
Dreaming of days and starry nights.
"Just imagine," it said with glee,
"Dancing through the urban spree!"

Leafy laughter fills the air,
With jokes that float like a gentle flair.
City greens found their own way,
In this bustling, fun-filled play!

Nature's Gentle Revolution

Tiny green troops in a pot parade,
Marching with glee in the sun-drenched shade.
"Who needs soil?" the sprouts declare,
"We'll thrive on laughter and fresh city air!"

Basil shouts, "It's time to grow!"
As others cheer, "We're ready, let's go!"
They plot and scheme for the sun's warm bite,
An uprising of greens in the golden light.

With each new leaf, they raise their arms,
"Nature's revolution has its charms!"
In pots they giggle and poke their foes,
The tough little sprouts that continue to grow!

So stand aside, all city-dwellers,
These cheeky greens are nature's yellers.
In bright sunshine, their laughter so sweet,
Join the merriment, take a seat!

Whispers of Green Beneath the Glass

In a pot with dirt so slight,
A sprout winks at the morning light.
It stretches tall, but oh so shy,
"I'm not a weed!" it laughs—oh my!

A rogue bug lands, feels like a king,
On tiny leaves, it starts to sing.
The plant just rolls its leaf-filled eyes,
"You're just a guest, now say goodbye!"

Neighbors stare, who'd think they'd gawk?
At quirky greenery, in the block.
It offers shade for bees and flies,
With whispers soft and leafy sighs.

So if you pass down our small street,
Don't giggle at my flora's feat.
What seems so lame and out of place,
Is just a plant with style and grace!

Sunlight's Embrace in Tiny Pots

In pots so small, they vie for sun,
Each leaf unfurls, 'Let's have some fun!'
One sprout declares, "I'm on a roll!"
The other laughs, "More like a shoal!"

Bursting forth in colors bright,
Eager to bask in golden light.
"Catch me if you can!" they shout and cheer,
As shadows dance and disappear.

A watering can's a jester here,
Spilling water, never fear!
Tiny roots wiggle with delight,
"We're all growing! It's quite the sight!"

As neighbors pass with casual glance,
The pots all do a little dance.
For what's a garden but a parade?
With sunlit smiles, it's all displayed!

Silent Bloom in Urban Spaces

Amidst the concrete, life springs forth,
A flower's mission, proving worth.
"Look at me!" it booms so bold,
"I'm not a weed, I'm pure gold!"

Between the bricks, the colors pop,
A showdown where the city's nonstop.
"Oh, don't you dare!" it cries in glee,
"No traffic can stop a sprout like me!"

A squirrel wanders, looking confused,
"Why's this lil' guy so amused?"
"Hey buddy, I'm just having fun,
I'm thriving here, I cannot run!"

So toast to blooms defying fate,
A testament we celebrate.
For what's a city without a green?
A dull retreat, not fit for scenes!

The Reach of Tender Leaves

Cradled snug in windows' glow,
Leaves reach out, oh, what a show!
"Hang ten, dude!" a leaf will say,
"Let's catch some rays, and then we play!"

With every sip of summer air,
They twist and turn without a care.
"I'm taller than you!" one boasts so loud,
While others giggle, feeling proud.

The gardener peeks, with eyes so wide,
His plants are having quite the ride.
"Next year, I'll need a bigger pot,
If you all keep this up, a lot!"

So if you see them in your time,
Those sprightly greens, oh so sublime.
Just know they're plotting, there's no doubt,
A leafy party—come check it out!

Beneath a Glassy Shield

Tiny sprouts in pots so round,
Crested leaves, a quirky mound.
Sunlight dances, shadows tease,
Water fights, Oh, plant with ease!

Mismatched pots, a lively crew,
Cacti gossip, herbs debut.
Fungus giggles, roots in play,
Who will thrive by end of day?

Basil dreams of pesto fame,
While mint claims a celebrity name.
Beans jump high, despite their size,
A sprout's ambition, the ultimate prize!

Beneath that glass, the circus thrives,
In this living, leafy hive.
Pocket-sized plants, they seem to race,
To conquer the sill, in leafy grace!

Cultivating Chaos

Sticky fingers, muddy thrills,
Planters tipped over, oh, the spills!
Seeds go flying, one in my hair,
This plant dad's a real millionaire!

Daisies laugh at my fine plan,
While daisies plot to be the man.
Thyme whispers jokes to wayward peas,
As parsley fledges like the breeze!

Weeds are rascals, spies galore,
In this green room, a leafy chore.
Sunshine peeks to lend a hand,
While I navigate this jungle land!

Tools laid out, a sight to see,
Gardening gloves, oh, woe is me!
But in this mess, I've found my groove,
With every gaffe, the plants improve!

Green Journeys

In little pots, where dreams are spun,
A sprout sneezes, and we all run.
Traveling soil, a sandy trip,
The blooms count down, 'Let's take a dip!'

Herbs are plotting world cuisine,
While ferns internaut, sleek and lean.
Each leaf unfurls, like a visa pass,
Stretched to the sun, with joy they amass!

Chasing raindrops, they leap and dive,
In this pot, they feel alive.
Petunias' gossip, oh, what a thrill,
As green pals quantum jump with zeal!

Roots may tangle, a tangled mess,
But friendship sprouts, we must confess.
In this haven, of pots and soil,
We cultivate joy, amid the toil!

The Art of Patience

Watch me water, a careful spill,
As I ponder the art of still.
Flora winks, a sly little tease,
Roots think hard, 'Oh please, oh please!'

Waiting for flowers, oh, what a task,
This leafy plea, none dare to ask.
Mint keeps mum, in a leafy stare,
While fern asks 'Do you think we're rare?'

A glimmer of hope in the sunlight's beam,
As sprouts take their time, just like a dream.
Patience wears a leafy crown,
As we giggle at this green showdown!

In the end, we dance with days,
Overjoyed in our quirky ways.
Beneath glass shields, the magic flows,
As every bloom crafts its own prose!

A Dance of Light and Life

Little plants in pots, oh so neat,
Bowing to the sun, they tap their feet.
With a wink and a wiggle, they sway,
Who knew foliage could dance all day?

A tomato plant dreams of becoming a feast,
While herb pals joke, 'We're the flavor beast!'
The daisies gossip, petals in a whirl,
In this leafy party, they giggle and twirl.

Nature's Refuge Amidst Stone

Cracks in the concrete, where green pokes through,
A cactus hums softly, 'I'm a spiky guru!'
While a fern whispers secrets to the wall,
'Life's a wild ride; just heed the call!'

A brave little sprout, bold as can be,
Shouts, 'I'll grow taller than you ever dreamed me!'
With roots so determined and leaves all a-flutter,
They juggle with raindrops and laugh at the clutter.

Resilience in Ruffled Leaves

Wind gives a tussle to the pot by the stairs,
Plants hold on tight, with leafy glares!
'You won't unseat us, you gusty foe!'
Ruffled and raucous, they put on a show.

'Look at me,' boasts the basil with flair,
'I'm here for the pizza, not just for air!'
The aloe, quite sassy, replies with a grin,
'Just wait for the sun, the real fun begins!'

Sprouts of Joy in Hidden Nooks

Beneath the sink, a rogue onion grin,
'Who knew I'd sprout? Now let's begin!'
Coffee mugs turned planters, who would have thought?
In this quirky garden, laughter can't be bought.

A stray herb's confession with a sly little nod,
'Life's a mixed salad, all tossed up by God!'
Between spoons and cups, joy starts to sprout,
In tiny, tight places, that's what it's about!

Shifts in the Seasons

Tiny leaves dance in the breeze,
A sprout is wearing little skis.
Just yesterday, they were so shy,
Now they reach up to the sky.

The sun sneezed, the rain giggled too,
As carrots plotted a sneaky coup.
Tomatoes wear their sassy hats,
While peas start forming gossip chats.

The Quiet Strength of Saplings

Little trees, with roots held tight,
Play peekaboo in morning light.
Wind whispers tales of dreamy nights,
As they stretch high in playful fights.

They giggle when the insects roam,
Polishing leaves, they feel like home.
With each new leaf, a secret's spun,
'We're the best, just look at us run!'

Miracles in Tiny Spaces

A flower peeks from the old shoe,
Saying, 'Look at my dazzling view!'
In such a nook, how can it thrive?
It sprouted forth, feeling so alive!

Butterflies cheer, it's quite the sight,
A garden party starts tonight!
With crickets tapping their tiny feet,
Nature's laughter is quite the treat!

Living Portraits of Hope

Painted pots with colors bright,
Cacti posing, oh, what a sight!
With beads of water like jewels fair,
Sketching dreams in the thin air.

A chubby herb, snuggled and plump,
Claims, 'I'm a sage, not just a lump!'
While daisies giggle in a row,
Each one says, 'We steal the show!'

A Symphony in Chlorophyll

In the sunlight they pirouette,
Each leaf a dancer, don't forget.
With pots as stages, roots so spry,
They wave their arms, reaching for the sky.

A tiny sprout with dreams so grand,
Wants to conquer every land.
But when the wind blows, oh how they sway,
Like they're in a waltz, come what may.

The sun sings loudly, a cheerful tune,
While raindrops join as the afternoon.
They jig and jive, all green and bright,
A leafy concert, pure delight.

So here's a show from nature's lot,
With growth and laughter, what a plot!
In pots galore, the fun is real,
A verdant symphony, what a deal!

From Soil to Sky

A bean sprout dreams of tall heights,
While ants laugh at its growth fights.
"Out of the ground!" they chant with glee,
"Just a bit more, you'll touch the trees!"

One morning, it stretches wide and bold,
Proclaims, "From dirt, I will unfold!"
The snails applaud, in their slow parade,
"Keep going up, don't be afraid!"

The sun blinks down with a wink and grin,
Poking fun at this leafy kin.
"Reaching for clouds is quite the feat,
But watch your step, don't make a mistake!"

So on they climb, a risqué affair,
Chasing the wind, light as air.
In nature's game, they take their shot,
From the earth they leap—like it or not!

The Promise of Petals

A bud declares it's time to bloom,
With petals bright, it clears the room.
But butterflies tease, flapping their wings,
"Show us your colors, oh, the joy it brings!"

It trembles a bit, then takes a chance,
With a flashy twirl, it joins the dance.
"Ta-da!" it beams, all dressed in hues,
While bees arrive, chanting the news.

"Look at the splendor!" the daisies shout,
As the roses laugh, "What's this all about?"
A crazy parade of floral cheer,
Spreading the joy as springtime's near.

With colors bright and scents so sweet,
Nature's comedians can't be beat.
Together they giggle, a floral spree,
In the land of petals, wild and free!

Nature's Small Wonders

A sprout in a pot thinks it's a tree,
"Just wait and see, the world is for me!"
But a snail zooms by, laughing with glee,
"Scale it back, buddy, just wait and see!"

The herbs in their planters are plotting a heist,
While a daisy rolls eyes, "This could be nice!"
They dream of adventures beyond the glass,
"Oh, to escape!" they all shout with sass.

A pint-sized garden, where chaos prevails,
Tiny leaves chase dreams in whimsical trails.
"Who knew we could be such a squad?"
Said the basil to mint, "Aren't we quite odd?"

With a sprinkle of water, and a dash of mirth,
They bask in the sun, their patch of earth.
Together they thrive, with laughter on hand,
Nature's small wonders, a kooky band!

Nourished by the Light

A plant in a pot, with leaves that flip,
Far from the ground, it takes a trip.
Stretching for sun, every little ray,
Its ambitions are grand, in a leafy ballet.

Sipping from droplets that fall from the sky,
It jokes with the beetles, oh my, oh my!
Chasing the shadows, making them dance,
This little green fella, just loves to prance.

The cat gives a glare, all judgmental and sly,
While our brave little sprout just smiles and sighs.
With curled-up fingers looking for fun,
Who's the real king when the day's almost done?

So here on the sill, life's silliness grows,
In pots of pure laughter, where mischief bestows.
A sing-song of nature, in its own quirky way,
Telling us stories of each sunny day.

Beyond the Frame

Peeking through glass, what wonders await,
A tiny green trophy, that just won first-rate.
With leaves like confetti, it celebrates cheer,
Watching the world from its safe little sphere.

The sun starts to snooze, and the shadows come out,
Our hero is ready, oh what a clout!
With roots intertwined, it declares, "I'm here!",
A champion of silliness, far from all fear.

Sipping on sunshine, and soaking up smiles,
It plans grand adventures, oh, the miles!
Just a leafy warrior, armed with delight,
Having a dance-off with dust motes at night.

From its wooden throne, it claims all it sees,
A throne fit for kings, and for plants with degrees.
With a wink to the moon, it giggles with glee,
This sprightly green fellow, so wild and so free!

Bloom Where You Are

In a humble pot, sits a curious sprout,
With ambitions so wild, it's starting to shout.
"Who needs the garden? I'm thriving just fine!"
As it winks at the thyme, it knows it will shine.

Tangled with tendrils, in a race to grow tall,
Daring the neighbor plants, 'I'm catching it all!'
While others look down, feeling quite small,
Our hero's convinced, it's destined to ball.

Chasing the sunset, it reaches for gold,
While grinning at sunbeams, bold stories unfold.
Swaying with laughter, in each little breeze,
Oh to be a plant, doing just as you please!

With leaves in a twist, making friends with the dust,
In the spotlight of radiance, it simply must trust.
"Bloom where you are! I'm the life of the show!"
In its pot of adventure, it just lets it glow!

The Symphony of Life's Cycles

On the edge of the sill, a concert begins,
Where vines play their harps, while the sunlight wins.
The wind offers beats, with a gentle flop,
As petals collide in a giggling plop.

Roots deep with stories, of trips to the moon,
While soil chats softly, hums a tune.
The rhythm of rain drops falls in parade,
And leaves rustle proudly, their dancing displayed.

Every sprout's a note in this wacky refrain,
With flowers that blossom, from laughter and rain.
The cabbage is groovy, the daisies can jive,
In this leafy orchestra, all feel alive.

So grab your own pot, join the quirky show,
Let's make some music, let our spirits grow!
In this symphony fine, every plant has its part,
Playing the melodies straight from the heart.

Love Letters to the Light

Dear sunshine, I'm a fan,
You brighten me with your tan.
Our love blooms like a sprout,
What's that smell? Oh, it's a clout!

I write to you, sweet rays so fine,
I'm a flower with a cheeky spine.
Do come visit, I'm quite spry,
But don't roast me, I might cry!

In the morning, I wave so glad,
Without you, I'd be quite mad.
Please don't stay away too long,
Or I'll wilt and that feels wrong!

So here's my note, quite sincere,
With love from this rooted dear.
Let's not let our joy grow dim,
Together we'll always win!

Potted Promises

I promised I wouldn't forget,
To water you when the sun's a threat.
But instead I spilled that can,
Now you're swimming, isn't it grand?

So here I sit, hope in my eyes,
Did I water or just cause cries?
You're now a plant with poolside views,
I'll blame the cat for your blues!

My green thumb seemed so spry,
But watering's an art—not a pie.
Next week, I'll try not to drown,
You'll be the king of this little town!

With all my jokes, don't take offense,
In this pot, I'll build suspense.
Here's a promise, fresh and crisp,
I'll give you care—just not a lisp!

Nature's Embrace

Oh, tiny leaf, you make me glee,
Clinging tight and wild and free.
Nature's hug around you weaves,
Pull that sunlight, oh how it leaves!

With morning light, you stretch and sway,
Dance with dust bunnies, come what may.
You giggle when the breeze blows by,
Sending seeds on a giggly fly.

When rain drops down, you splash about,
Like a toddler—I have no doubt.
So let's embrace this wacky ride,
With pollen laughter as our guide!

Together we bask, just you and me,
In this wild wacky, leafy spree.
So grab your sunlight, grab your fun,
Nature found, the frolic begun!

A Breath of Fresh Beginnings

With a puff of air, I sprout my dreams,
In a pot filled with giggly themes.
Roots tickle, stretch way down below,
I'll dance on this sill, watch me glow!

I catch a breeze, it whispers sweet,
"Grow taller, my friend, never admit defeat!"
So upwards I climb, in my tiny world,
With aspirations like leaves unfurled.

My life's a party, come join the spree,
Where plants can laugh and be silly like me.
A new leaf is born, take a deep whiff,
I promise, I'm no withered tiff!

So here's a toast to fresh, bright starts,
With roots and giggles, we play our parts.
Let's chuckle at life, my leafy mate,
In this pot of joy, oh isn't it great?

Whispering Sprouts

Tiny leaves poke up with glee,
Reaching out for coffee, you see.
Whispering secrets, oh what a show,
I think they're plotting, but don't tell the crow.

A plant's inner monologue, who could have guessed?
Chasing sunlight while I still rest.
If only they knew how loud they could be,
Shhh, quiet, my leafy friends, let me watch TV!

They stretch and they wiggle, a comical sight,
Balancing each other as if in a fight.
The basil flirts with the vibrant chive,
How do these plants seem so much more alive?

If they could walk, this I know,
They'd dance in the breeze, put on a show.
With pots as their stage, a lively scene,
Next door, the tomatoes roll their eyes, routine!

The Dance of New Beginnings

Under the sun's warm embrace,
Little green dancers claim their space.
They jiggle and sway, oh what a trance,
Inviting the flies to join in the dance!

Each sprout is a whirling, giggling sprite,
Who knew that plants could be this polite?
With roots in the soil, they practice their moves,
They spin and they twirl, look at them groove!

The soil claps softly, a rhythmic beat,
As tiny hands wave, isn't this sweet?
They laugh and they cheer, though I can't quite hear,
Hoping the neighbor brings popcorn near!

So here in my haven, they put on a show,
With dreams of sunshine, and even some snow.
If plants were to party, I'd definitely stay,
With snacks and some water, let's groove the day!

Life Between the Glass

Peeking through the panes, they signal, "Hello!"
Tiny green faces ready to grow.
Drama unfolds in a bath of light,
Who will reach up for their chance to take flight?

The spider plant giggles, oh what a tease,
While succulents bask as if in a breeze.
A rivalry brews, who'll capture the sun?
They trade barbs like children, it's all in good fun!

In pots lined up neatly, the tales intertwine,
Who's growing taller, who's sipping more wine?
The ferns roll their eyes, "We're classy and cool,"
While the herbs snicker softly, "This isn't a school!"

So, here's to the chaos and life in a jar,
Where silliness thrives, and jokes travel far.
With laughter and sunlight, they plug into space,
In this glass-bound circus, all find their place!

A Green Haven Within

A sanctuary blooms, in colors so bold,
With characters growing, each story unfolds.
Cacti wear armor, oh what a tough crew,
While daisies spin tales of romance and dew!

A rumor is whispered, "Did you see how I sprout?"
With petals that flutter and roots that flout.
Moss giggles back, "You think you're a star?"
In the quirky green kingdom, they all raised the bar!

Little sprouts bicker, who's hottest this year?
Role-playing plants with their favorite cheers.
"Watch us all flourish, we're savvy and keen!"
Life's a potluck, each tends to their green!

From snappy puns to the quirks that they share,
This leafy abode is beyond compare.
Together they flourish, an oddball brigade,
In laughter and sunlight, their worries all fade!

The Journey of a Seed

Once a little seed had a grand dream,
To sprout up high and be on the team.
He wriggled and jiggled, oh what a sight,
But faced a great challenge, a snail in the night.

With moss on his back, the snail took a stroll,
And our tiny seed shouted, "Dude, let me roll!"
They laughed and they danced, became quite a pair,
Two friends on a journey, full of laughter to share.

The sun shone bright, and the rain fell just right,
Our seed grew its roots, oh what pure delight!
"I'm not just a snack!" he said with a cheer,
"I'm blooming with style, watch out, I'm here!"

So here's to the seeds, and their quirky little plight,
Try not to be slow, let your dreams take flight!
For in tiny little packages, wild tales do sprout,
Seeds, once with a dream, now are legends, no doubt.

Nature's Resilience Within

A cactus in a corner, oh so prickly and bold,
Whispered to the fern, "Together we're gold!"
They plotted adventures, with sunlight as their guide,
While the poor little spider just wanted to hide.

The fern said, "Let's dance!" The cactus replied,
"Only if you promise not to get snide!"
With a sway and a wiggle, they caused quite a fuss,
While the spider rolled eyes, all caught in the bus.

Pigeons cooed loudly, "It's nature's grand show!"
As the flowers all giggled, putting on a glow.
Our friends laughed and sang, under skies so blue,
Even rocks wanted in on the fun too!

So nature, in all her silly little ways,
Turns laughter to leaves, in the sun's warm rays.
These greens talk and play, despite the frowns we give,
In their zany little world, they truly do live!

A Pocket of Paradise

In a pot by the window, where sunlight beams,
Lived a plant named Fred, chasing funny dreams.
With leaves made of glitter, and roots of pure gold,
He fancied himself a knight, brave and bold.

His ally, a spider, spinning webs with flair,
Said, "Fred, go grab water! Show 'em you care!"
But Fred had a vision, a grand plant parade,
Where neighbors would cheer, and the sun made the grade.

When watering day came, the serious drill,
Fred wiggled his leaves, thought "This is a thrill!"
With a splash and a splash, he danced like a star,
Spritzing his friends, saying, "Look how we spar!"

A pocket of giggles, a paradise neat,
Where each little leaf had a funny repeat.
For in Fred's funny realm, from soil to the sky,
Every day's a party; oh my, oh my!

Spirit of the Sprout

Once a cautious sprout peered out at the sun,
Wondering, "Will I match the flowers—everyone?"
With a bounce in her leaves, she waved to the breeze,
"Cheers to being weird; let's go and tease the trees!"

"I'll be a tulip!" she cried with delight,
"Or a dancing daisy, all dressed up so bright!"
The herb next door chuckled, "You do what you crave,
Just know in this garden, we all act so brave!"

Then came the rain, with thunderous applause,
"Don't hide!" yelled the weeds, "Be chic without flaws!"
So the sprout threw a shindig, all roots in a bunch,
"Let's boogie till bedtime; let's all have a lunch!"

With petals in hand, and a twinkle of cheer,
The spirit of sprouting knows no bounds here.
So next time you see something tiny and small,
Remember, with laughter, they're standing up tall!

Echoes of Nature's Resilience

Tiny sprouts in a tiny pot,
Waging war against the rot.
Silly leaves with a sunny grin,
Sway like dancers, let the fun begin!

Pushed by rays of morning light,
Shouting, 'Hey, we're growing right!'
Whispers in the soil below,
Remind them that they steal the show.

With roots that tickle, chase, and tease,
They're plotting mischief on the breeze.
A game of chase with a passing fly,
While sitting snug, they wave goodbye!

So on this ledge, in pots so bright,
Laughter sprouts from morning's light.
Nature's jests, a colorful riddle,
In the garden of a windowsill.

Tapestry of Verdure at Dawn

A quirky plant in a sunlit zone,
Asserts its claim, 'This is my throne!'
Leaves that giggle, shifts that sway,
Up above, they're on display!

The cactus sleeps with quirky dreams,
Wishing for coffee and fun-filled schemes.
Chuckle at neighbors spreading wide,
While little ferns do a happy glide.

Sunbeams tickle each leafy friend,
Tick-tock, the morning fun won't end.
Each petal hums a silly tune,
Promising joy by afternoon!

In this tapestry, laughter blooms,
Amidst the pots and sunny rooms.
A delightful show in leafy attire,
Where every twist is sure to inspire!

Fragments of Eden on a Ledge

In a sprawling kingdom made of clay,
Leaves convene and they love to play.
A basil dancing, a mint doing tricks,
While tiny daisies laugh at their picks.

A window's edge, a party place,
Herbs in costumes, full of grace.
'Who's the tallest?' calls out the thyme,
A funny race amidst sunlight climbs!

Jumping little sprouts in their green attire,
Invite you in, all set for the choir.
With petals bursting, bursting with cheer,
Each whisper says, 'Come join us here!'

On this ledge, where stories combine,
Nature's antics, all intertwine.
A celebration of laughter and cheer,
In fragments of Eden, so near, so near!

Heartbeats of Flora in Stillness

In the stillness, giggles blare,
Pot-bound pals, a lively affair.
A dancing petal, a nodding sprout,
Whispering secrets that float about.

Roots intertwining in silly fights,
Claiming space with friendly bites.
Leaves like laughter, growing wide,
In this cozy nook, they side by side.

A sprinkle of soil, a dash of light,
Brewing mischief, such a sight!
While shadows play on the garden's floor,
Nature's heart beats; oh, what a roar!

In every moment, every embrace,
From soft green cheeks to a vibrant space.
Here, stillness dances, laughter swirls,
In this real-life tale of leafy girls!

www.ingramcontent.com/pod-product-compliance
Lightning Source LLC
Chambersburg PA
CBHW070329120526
44590CB00017B/2836